For Margaret

MEMORIES

A PICTORIAL CELEBRATION FOR DUBLIN'S MILLENNIUM

Compiled and Edited by **John Coughlan**

Published by **Smurfit Publications Ltd.**
in association with **John Coughlan**

Captions & Research: **Shay Healy** and John Coughlan

Design: **Des Kiely & Associates**

Cover photograph hand tinted by **Amelia Stein**

Typesetting: **The Caseroom**

Origination: **Litho Colour Plates**

Printed by **Richview Browne & Nolan** in the Republic of Ireland.

The publishers wish to acknowledge with sincere thanks the help and assistance of the following individuals and organisations in compiling the collection of photographs for this book: John Kennedy; Michael O'Reilly; Aer Lingus and Phil Newport; Bord Failte and Paddy Tutty; Cork Examiner and Stephen Coughlan, Donal Crosbie, Tim O'Brien; Michael Corcoran and the Transport Museum, Howth; Jim Connelly; City Hall Archives and Mary Clark; Dublin Civic Museum and Patrick Johnston; Cyril Ferris; the Guinness Group and Peter Walsh; Hot Press Magazine; The Irish Press Group and Liam Flynn; National Library (Lawrence and Eason Collections); Lensmen; Royal Dublin Society and David Grey; RTE and Brelda Baum; UCD Irish Folklore Department and Barbara O'Floinn; Zoological Gardens and Terry Murphy.

Photographs on pages 20, 21 (Cashman Collection), 22, 23, 24, 25 (Murtagh Collection), 68, 69, 70, 71, 80, 81, 82, 83 Courtesy of RTE Library.

The Jefferson Smurfit Group plc

Foreword

Dublin has inspired the publication of a vast number of books about its "rare auld times," and not so rosy-hued ones. The vast Lawrence Collection of early photographs, taken throughout Ireland between 1870 and 1910, and now housed in the National Library has been trawled again and again for pictures to pad out books about Old Dublin. And indeed, it proved to be an invaluable source of material to illustrate the earliest period of city life recorded in Memories.

Many other photographs, including that dramatic one of union leader Jim Larkin caught in full oratorical flight, during the bitter Lockout of 1913, may also seem familiar.

But **Memories** is not a new book of previously unpublished photographs, or a new book of reworked published photographs; rather the first book to draw on so many sources, to put Dublin and Dubliners more or less fully in the picture. . . from the early days of photography to the present time.

Memories is intended to jog them. Few, if any, living Dubliners will remember the horse drawn trams which whisked the citizens through the streets broad and narrow (probably more rapidly than the traffic jammed buses of today) in the second half of the 19th century. But many will remember the electric trams which, in increasingly sophisticated forms, were part of the city streetscapes until 1949.

Memories recalls those milestone events of 20th Century Dublin: The 1911 visit of King George V – the last reigning British monarch to set a royal foot in this part of Ireland; the 1916 Rising and the destruction of the city centre in its suppression; the night the Luftwaffe bombed the capital of neutral Ireland; the homecoming of the Irish American heroes – John F. Kennedy and Princess Grace (Kelly); the visits of Pope John Paul and Presidents Nixon and Reagan; curtain call for the "The Pillar," the city's most famous landmark, and the passing of Eamonn de Valera, the country's most famous citizen; the terrible tragedy of the Stardust fire.

But everyday moments get equal billing with the big events in **Memories**; particularly through the photographs of Neville Johnson, an artist-photographer, who wandered the streets, lanes and markets of Dublin with his camera during 1952 and 1953.

Some Dublin institutions – the Zoo, the Guinness Brewery, the Royal Dublin Society, Radio Telefis Eireann-merited special little sections of their own; while those pictures of the city's sporting heroes will recall some very proud and happy memories for native Dubliners.

While **Memories** is mainly a photographic collection to celebrate the city's 1000th birthday; it also includes a selection of personal tributes by a cross section of prominent citizens, representing different professions, who agreed to share with us their own personal memories of their city.

The generous sponsorship of the Jefferson Smurfit Group has enabled us to share all the Memories of this book, with native and adopted Dubliners and Millennium visitors alike, in a lasting hardback format – for the price of a paperback. We would like to think that our **Memories** of Dublin will endure.

John Coughlan

CONTENTS

The flower seller, Moore Street.

Westmoreland Street, looking towards O'Connell Street in the 1880's. This fine broad street prepared the traveller for the expanse of O'Connell Street, Europe's widest boulevard.

The elegant western frontage of Trinity College, designed by Henry Keene and John Sanderson of London and built between 1752 – 1759, is the perfect backdrop for a non-rush hour view of the horse-drawn traffic on College Green, circa the 1880's.

The skyline of Grafton Street, circa 1880's. Little has changed since. Note the pair of Union Jacks and the Trocadero Restaurant, in the building which now houses the Allied Irish Bank. ▶

Main Street, Blackrock Village, five miles from Dublin. The lone motorcar gives no indication of the bottle-neck this street will become in later years.

Strand Road, Sandymount, circa 1900. Sandymount Tower is in the background. Gas lamps still stand amongst the new-fangled electric lamp standards. The horse drawn carts pass either side of the No. 3 tram.

O'Connell Street and Eden Quay are alive with people, in this streets scene, circa 1880's. There appears to have been little regard for lane discipline. ▶

EDEN QUAY. DUBLIN 3114. W.L.

Long, long ago, you could get on yer bike and go for a sedate spin past St. Stephen's Green up in the direction of Harcourt Street. Today, those three demurely dressed young lady cyclists would be swept to their deaths by a tidal wave of one-way traffic.

One hundred years ago, Dubliners enjoyed a day at the seaside every bit as much as they do today. Come to think of it, the clothes they wore then were really much better suited to Irish summer weather than the 20th century bikini This summer parade of the 1880's was recorded in front of the Marine Station Hotel in Bray.

Rush hour at Kelly's Corner circa 1910. ▶

At the end of the 19th century Howth Village nestles like a jewel at the foot of the Hill of Howth. In the background is Ireland's Eye, a rocky island one mile from the shore.

An exchange of gossip on the pier of the inner harbour at Kingstown, now known as Dun Laoghaire. The Royal Mail Boat is docked in the background. ▶

Dublin suburban towns and villages had a heart when these pictures were taken in the early part of the century. Kingstown (Dun Laoghaire), Malahide, Ranelagh and Rathfarnham have since been absorbed by the outbound march of greater Dublin. But all four retain a good deal of their special character.

Main Street, Kingstown.

Main Street, Malahide.

ON MAIN STREET

Main Street, Ranelagh.

Main Street, Rathfarnham.

Chamber Street circa 1911. Dubliners called this type of architecture, "Dutch Billies" (after the style of old Amsterdam architecture), and associated the houses with the Huguenots and their weaving which had flourished in the Liberties.

Clothing stalls flourished in Patrick Street in 1896. They later moved to the covered Iveagh Market. On the left is the pub of PJ McCall, the "Bard of the Liberties."

The good old days? Very few of the children living on West Road in the North Strand area of Dublin owned shoes, when this picture was taken in 1910. ▶

George V was crowned King of England on June 22, 1911. In one of his first trips overseas, King George and Queen Mary paid a visit to Dublin from July 12-17th and festive crowds turned out to greet the Royal couple.

The 1916 Rising, which took place in Dublin during Easter Week, did not have much popular support amongst the populace of Dublin. The insurgents, the Irish Volunteers, occupied the General Post Office in O'Connell Street and declared a Republic. But shells from British gunboats anchored on the Liffey, proved so lethal that the Irish Commander-in-chief, Patrick H. Pearse surrendered "to prevent further slaughter of Dublin citizens." Sixteen leaders of the Rising were later executed.

Crowds congregate at Nelson's Pillar to view the damage. ▶

The Tramway Offices in O'Connell Street, which were badly damaged.

Curious crowds gather on O'Connell Street. The Carlton cinema is on the extreme right of the photograph.

The French Sisters of Charity with their distinctive headresses, dispensing bread to the poor, during the rising. ▶

Devastation in O'Connell Street, or Sackville Street as it was called at the time of the Rising.

Memories

Ronnie Delaney
Olympic Gold Medallist

*T*he locality where I grew up in Dublin, during the 40's and 50's, was a virtual sporting paradise. Let me explain. I loved all my young life in the suburb of Sandymount – "Melrose," 33, St. John's Road, to be exact. The house, or more precisely the road, was encircled by a plethora of sporting amenities. Directly behind were the seven grass courts of Claremont LTC and beyond them the expansive grounds of the Railway Union Sports Club encompassing in different seasons, hockey, rugby, soccer or cricket, tennis, bowls and athletics.

If I were to turn right coming out my front gate I could pass by the beautiful St. John the Evangelist Church and on to the composite grounds of Monkstown RFC and the Pembroke Cricket Club. If I chose to turn left coming out the gate I could walk but one hundred yards up to the Martello Tower. Beyond it stretched the expansiveness and fun of Sandymount Strand where each Summer I ran, swam poorly with one hand constantly on the bottom, perilously sailed my canoe or stabbed for flat fish. That's when we were not playing cricket on the sun dried sand after the tide obligingly went out as far as the eye could see.

Little surprise than that I loved many sports, played them all and grew up in sporting companionship with my pals from Park Avenue, Sydney Parade, Wilfield Road and the Green. We were all simply sports mad, spending every moment outside of school playing whatever sport was in season or vogue with all the enthusiasm and abandon of our youthful years.

We were brainwashed for all time, spending hours watching our sporting heroes of diverse codes, admiring them and learning to imitate their athletic skills by assiduously following their every move. We were inspired too by the magic of so many sporting occasions; rugby and hockey internationals at nearby Lansdowne on London Bridge Road, soccer matches when Dad took me to watch Rovers in Glenmalure Park along with the weekly home fixtures we automatically went to see to cheer on our teams.

There was no TV to distract us and only the weekly visit to the flics and the folleyer upper in the Shack gave the myriad pitches around Sandymount a respite from our pounding feet.

I am enthralled by all that is written today about the challenge of the new leisure revolution with increased free time. The media and various agencies constantly exhort us to be active, to come alive for health's sake or as an antidote to crime or juvenile delinquency. Let's recapture what I enjoyed with my pals the Tanhams and the Gallaghers in the Sandymount of old.

Things were never as good as today. Railway, Monkstown, Claremont all survive with spanking new facilities and amenities. The Corpo have improved the Strand almost beyond recognition with mile after beautiful mile of landscaped promenades. Herbert Park features outstanding sporting amenities including hard tennis courts, bowling and now a croquet lawn, paralleling similar amenities in all the fine parks of our lovely city from St. Annes to Bushy Park, to Blackrock, the Phoenix Park and so on. Dublin Corporation can be proud in how they are matching the challenge of the leisure revolution. It's all there in our beautiful city. Look around. See the beautiful flowers, lawns and trees in all our city parks.

One way or another, do visit Sandymount, the loveliest village in the city, where fifty years on I still bank, get my dry cleaning done and where John Duffy, the local gentlemen's hairdresser on Seafort Avenue for nigh on forty years, remains immune to the effects of inflation; charging a little over a quid for a short back and sides with nothing extra for his friendship and chat.

Memories

Gay Byrne
Broadcaster

I *grew up on the South Circular Road in Dublin, around the area of Dolphins Barn, Cork Street and the meeting of the two canals; just on the edge of The Liberties.*

It was at the tail end of the tenement era and the growth of the new areas like Crumlin, Drimnagh and Kimmage.

The exodus from the rat-infested squalor of inner Dublin was well under way to the new dormitory suburbs, almost within touching-distance of the Dublin Mountains.

At Herberton Bridge, three hundred yards from my home, the Madigan family had a farm, where we bought potatoes, cabbage, beans and peas straight out of the ground; and we gave our kitchen waste to them to feed their pigs.

That entire farm is now Fatima Mansions.

I went to sleep to the sound of the canal barges putt-putting their way from Guinness's basin to Athy and Shannon Harbour and other mysterious places.

I remember the trams lines being removed from the South Circular Road and the day the buses came on the route for the first time. The streets were crowded with people to greet them.

They were the days of Bang-Bang and Fortycoats and Stab-the-Rasher and a whole menagerie of odd oul' wans and oul' fellas who were best avoided if you were young

and impressionable. The entire period is superbly recreated in Lar Redmond's book "Emerald Square" – which was just down Cork Street from Dolphins Barn.

In my day, the South Circular Road was considered quite upmarket and a desirable place to live. Now, whenever I pass that way, I am depressed at the extent to which it has become flatland and the world of the bedsit, and it all seems smaller and cramped and rather run-down.

The Rialto Cinema, outside of which I seemed to spend half my life queueing for the fourpenny rush, is now a car salesroom; and the Leinster Cinema, where I spent the other half, is an ice rink. Most of the other regular dream-houses are long since gone. For when things were flush, and a few extra bob appeared from nowhere, then the thrill of thrills was to end up in The Metropole, The Capitol, The Regal or The Theatre Royal. Ask your granny – she'll tell you about them.

The summer queues for the bus to take us to Harcourt Street Station; then the queue for the steamy monster to take us to Bray and the seaside.

The thrill, the anticipation; the excitement and the tiredness coming home.

Our kids have it all too easy, with the result – they appreciate nothing. When nobody had anything; little things meant a lot.

In the aftermath of the 1916 Rising, random roadblocks became part of everyday life on the streets of Dublin.

This historic photograph shows the take over of Dublin Castle by the Irish police, the Civic Guards, at 1.30 p.m. on the afternoon of August 17th, 1922.►

Michael Collins coffin is borne on a gun carriage through the streets of Dublin.

Arthur Griffith was editor of the United Irishman and founder of Sinn Fein – "We Ourselves." He led the delegation which negotiated the Anglo-Irish Treaty of 1921 and he subsequently was elected President of the Irish Free State when De Valera resigned. On June 28, 1922, Civil War broke out between Free Staters and Republicans. Griffith died on August 12th, 1922 and a huge crowd turned out for his funeral through the streets of the capital. Amongst the mourners was Griffiths Pro-Treaty colleague and Commander of the Government Forces, General Michael Collins. Ten days later Collins himself was dead, killed in an ambush by Republicans at Beal na mBlath, between Macroom and Bandon in Co. Cork. ▶

In 1905 the driver and conductor of this electric tram posed for a picture to mark the extension of the College Green-Drumcondra service to Whitehall.

Back in 1880, the cry FIRE! brought this impressive body of men of the Inchicore Fire Brigade rushing to the rescue with their gleaming fire fighting equipment.

Before the opening of the Blessington Tramway, the one horsepower of the Blessington Mail offered the fastest means of escape to the mountains from the hurly burly of life in the city centre. These gents were setting off from the Princess Street terminus (beside the GPO) in the early 1870's. ▶

DUBLIN ON WHEELS

A Napier Charabanc pictured in Kingstown around 1912. The passengers appear to be of some importance judging by the send off.

In the late 1920's Corkonians taking the one way journey to Dublin could arrive refreshed after a good night's sleep on the road. But the Sleeper Omnibus Service did not catch on and was soon discontinued.

A day at the seaside? Wherever they were going these girls from a Dublin city orphanage were looking forward (despite the crush) to their day out in a Charabanc of the Garryowen Transport Company. They were pictured with their minders, who appear to have to have looked to Chicago for their dress sense, in North William Street in 1926. ▶

On the day of its takeover by Dublin United Tramways, the entire fleet of the Wicklow Hills Bus Company was lined up outside the Powerscourt Arms for this historic picture.

A Dublin city "pirate" bus of the early 1930's. After World War 1 "pirate" buses battled with the tram companies for the fares of the city's commuters. The "pirates" soon began to pool their resources and form co-ops, which gave first the trams, and later the licenced bus companies a good run for their passengers. By 1936 most had disappeared or been absorbed by the big three – The Great Northern, Great Southern and Dublin United Tramways.

Privatisation is the buzz word of the late 1980's. So what are the chances of Dublin's "Corpo" again looking to the private sector to clean the city's streets and collect the refuse. This strange looking De Dion Bouton street washer belonged to Franco Irish Enterprises which had a contract to keep Dublin Squeaky clean between 1925 and the early 1940's ▶

There were not too many private cars competing with the trams when these pictures were taken of Dublin's main thoroughfare in the late 1920's.

O'Connell St. looked quite lively when this view was recorded in the year 1930. ▶

A total of four units of the Drum Battery train – designed by Dr. James Drum of Trinity College – were built, two in 1932, and two in 1939. They played a big role in maintaining a surburban rail service during "The Emergency". Picture shows a Drum Battery about to arrive into Foxrock station in 1950.

Dublin Area Rapid Transport (DART) was the answer to the city's traffic jams, at least in the coastal area. It went into service in 1984 and links the seaside suburban town of Bray in the south with the fishing village of Howth in the north city.

One hundred years after the rail link between Dublin and Cork was formally opened, majestic steam engines still dominated the country's tracks. The huge Centenary Express was pictured at Kingsbridge Station in 1949 before setting out on its commemoration run to Cork. ▶

DUBLIN
CORK

CENTENARY EXPRESS

800

Memories

Patrick J. Wright
M.D. Smurfit Ireland

Dublin has always been home to me. I was born and reared in Fairview and went to O'Connell Schools, North Richmond Street, for ten years. I courted and married a Dublin girl from Clontarf, and my first home was in Kilbarrack. As my mother and father were both also from Dublin, I suppose this makes me a "Jackeen."

My first memories of growing up in Dublin were of Fairview Park. Because my father owned a Fish & Poultry shop on the main thoroughfare in Fairview, we had no garden, either front or back, and my father used to say we had the biggest front garden in Ireland. Indeed we had.

Fairview Park, with its many football and hurling pitches, its trees to climb and bushes in which to play "hide and seek" and "relieveo", and of course a bandstand-where during the long summer evenings bands played and Irish dancing was performed. Many an "All Ireland" or "Soccer International" was played and won in Fairview Park against the "old enemy", St. Aidan's Park road, Carlton Road and Malahide Road.

When not in Fairview Park, the roads of Marino were a favourite haunt of the Haverty Road Gang, of which yours truly was the leader. Here we "boxed the fox" in various gardens, knocked on doors for jam-jars to get into the Fairview Grand for the Saturday afternoon matinee, where two large jam-jars would get you into the 'Fourpenny Rush" to see the "follierupper" of "Flash Gordon," "Captain Maravel" or "Hopalong Cassidy."

Sumertime saw us going to Dollymount for swims; we weren't allowed swim on the Howth side because of "curley's hole" (quicksand) and the Dublin side was always cold and much too deep for non-swimmers. The old Clontarf Baths were also a favourite haunt; if you could scrounge the money to get in. The Crescent in

Marino, which was exclusive to the residents of that particular area, offered us trees and bushes to play some great games of "relieveo" in, though we were always at odds with the lads from the area and weren't always allowed in to play.

For some strange reason I wasn't sent to St. Joseph's, Fairview, where all my friends went to school. My father instead sent me to O'Connell Schools, probably because it was his old Alma Mater, and there I spent ten not unhappy years learning the "Three R's". My mother often said if brains were in feet, I would have been a genius as I loved, and still do, Gaelic football and hurling. O'Connell Schools in those days was a very metropolitan school, with boys from all over the North side of Dublin attending. In my Leaving Class alone we had four priests, a famous surgeon, a well-known trade union official, and numerous successful businessmen.

My teenage years coincided with the Rock 'n' Roll era – Bill Hailey, Elvis Presley, Fats Domino, etc. The place to be on a Sunday night in Fairview was at the St. Vincent's Boxing Hall in Melrose Avenue. Looking back, it seems to me that three or four hundred rock 'n' rollers, with white sports coats, grease in their hair, rocked the night away. I had to be home at 11 o'clock, which meant it was difficult to get a "leave home." I wasn't allowed to go on the Wednesday night, as I was still in school. From Melrose Avenue we progressed to Home Farm, to Glasnevin Tennis Club, and to the C.Y.M.S. in Fairveiw, in that order. These were the days when an 8 o'clock start ensured queues at 7.30 p.m., and if you weren't a member you didn't get in. The "hard chaws" tried to get in after 10 o'clock when they had consumed a few pints. Drugs were unheard of. Nobody had a car.

And the fellow with the Lambretta scooter was King of the dancefloor.!

They were also the days when the girls were on one side, and the boys on the other side, with the girls in groups of three and four talking very earnestly to one another, not noticing "the lads" as they walked up and down their own side to see who they were going to ask up for the next dance. If you hadn't got your girl chosen by half-time, i.e. 10.30 p.m. when you offered a glass of orange and a packet of crisps, a "leave home" was very doubtful. As everyone lived close and nearby, walking home in those days didn't cause any problems. And you certainly had no problems with muggings or being attacked. These things didn't enter into the equation.

Sunday afternoons were usually Croke Park with my father to see every team, other than Dublin, until we hit the Golden Fifties. This is when St. Vincent's came into their own and produced a Dublin team with 14 Vincent's men and one man from Beann Eadair – the goalkeeper Paddy Flaherty. My heroes in those days were Kevin Heffernan, Ollie Freeney and Jim Lavin of Malahide Road, 'cause I knew him and delivered fish to his mother, and sometimes he'd even say hello!

Things have changed, or have they? I still go to Croke Park with my son on a Sunday. Instead of Fairview Park it's Malahide Castle Demesne. Swimming on Malahide beach. I suppose the major change is that the simplicity we enjoyed in my growing-up days in Dublin seem to have gone forever. O'Connell Street has changed dramatically. We worry about youthful drinking and, of course, that dreadful social scourge, drugs. One cannot window-shop as one did before in Dublin City without being pestered by someone looking for something or other. And the friendliness on the streets has changed, though the people in Dublin are still friendly.

Memories

Noel Pearson
Theatrical Impresario

A *few years ago, I produced a one-man show with Niall Toibín. The preamble to his story about Cork men and 'de Banks' was that Corkonians can get homesick even before they leave Cork! I suppose this is one of the few things the Dubs and the Corkonians have in common.*

Nevertheless, one of the most abiding memories I have as a child growing up in Dublin in the 50's was the night after Christmas, when there could be up to a dozen or more young men and women leaving from neighbouring houses for the night boat to Liverpool. The mothers and the younger family members wept and the fathers gave hard handshakes and away they went until summer or maybe the following Christmas. To-day it's America or Australia but they seem to come home more regularly.

Nowadays, it's quite fashionable to recall Dublin 'in the rare auld times' as a place populated by 'joxers', 'hard men' and 'hard chaws', when every pub between George's Street and Merrion Row had wall-to-wall poets, painters, novelists and assorted artistes. In the 50's I was too young to frequent the pubs, but I understand from a few of my older pals that the drinking writers, painters etc. would to-day (if they were about) howl with laughter at the mythology that has grown up about them.

It was the '60's before the ordinary Dub started to live. Then there was plenty of work and everybody seemed to be able to live a lot better on what they were paid. The architectural destruction of the city had not yet begun; the Metropole, Pillar, Red Bank, Hibernian, The Russell, the Royal and the wonderful Paradiso were all still there and

the ordinary Dub had, for the first time, a few bob to enjoy them.

It was the golden age of Lemass. We were being swept along by the social revolution that spread from Carnaby Street to Munich, and for me, music dominated the times and the Beatles dominated the music.

Here in this city, we had our own mini musical revolution. Five hard men, Ronnie, Luke, Ciaran, John and Barney – The Dubliners – turned ballads and folk music on its head. The crack was mighty and I was in my twenties enjoying every minute of it.

Dublin is a great city; small enough not to be too lonely, and big enough to get lost in, if you want to. Perhaps the city is a bit 'frayed at the cuffs' at the moment but she is clean; cleaner than most places I've been in.

Perhaps she needs a new hat and a pair of shoes. Perhaps . . . .!

However, is it not ironic that the city that gave Wilde, Yeats, Shaw, Joyce, Becket, O'Casey and Behan to the world, should have none of their houses restored or maintained and no statues, portraits, museums or galleries to honour them? Yet this woman, 'Anna Livia', with the great child-bearing hips, is about to give birth to a £200 million monument to mammon to be known as a Financial Services Centre.

Maybe the poor woman has been on her back for so long she has at last decided to charge for it.

Never mind, me auld flower, we're all still mad about you.

The St. Patrick's Day parade in Thomas Street (date unknown), outside St. Catherine's Church, the site where Robert Emmet was executed in 1798.

Islandbridge on the River Liffey. The coxed-fours battle it out on the water, as eager fans line the banks.

Last minute checks for the crew at Dublin University Regatta of 1927.▶

This was the Assembly Hall of the Royal Dublin Society, when it occupied Leinster House. It is now the Dail chamber where the Irish government conducts it's business of state.

In 1902, the seating capacity at the R.D.S. Horse Show was a mere 2,500. But what they lacked in numbers, they made up for in style.

Dublin Horse Show, 1908. The parade ring is full and a sizeable crowd enjoys the relaxed atmosphere.

The Governor-General, Tim Healy, Lord Powerscourt and the Maharajah of Alwar at the Horse Show in 1926.

The Dublin Horse Show at the R.D.S. Ballsbridge, 1923. Thomas Prior House is in the background.

The Dublin rag man made his living by recycling rags of all sorts. Sometimes he swapped small toys with children for rags they collected. This picture was taken by Maurice Curtin (copyright Folklore Dept. U.C.D.) was taken in a suburban housing estate in 1937.▶

The Eucharistic Congress of 1932, held in the Phoenix Park, attracted over a million people to Dublin. Festive bunting and decorations festooned the city and streets, like the one pictured on the right. A special shrine was built on O'Connell Bridge and the religious ceremonies took place on a specially built altar in the Phoenix Park.

The Dublin "blackout" during World War II was no
protection on the night of May 31st, 1941, when German
bombers mistook their target and dropped bombs on
Dublin's North Strand area. The Germans later
apologised for the incident, which cost the lives of 34
people and destroyed approximately three hundred houses.

O'Connell Street, 1940's. Bicycles predominate, but already the buses are replacing the trams. Horatio Nelson still proudly stands on his Pillar, having become the major terminus for Dublin's bus and tram transport.

A Summerhill street scene in 1952. ▶

Back in 1934 the Irish Air Corps trained its pilots to fly by the seat of their pants. The pilot of this contraption was *Johnny Mather* who went on to greater things as one of the first employees of Aer Lingus, set up two years later.

Robert Loraine, a well known actor, attempted to become the first man to fly the Irish Sea in September 1910. He took off from Anglesey in Wales in a pretty basic looking Farnam biplane; only to drop into the sea an hour later, just off the coast at Howth. He swam the last few yards to Ireland.

An early Irish bird man and a nutty professor to boot. That was Professor George Francis Fitzgerald. No doubt his students found his attempts to take wings from the grounds of Trinity College in 1895 vastly more entertaining than his lectures. ▶

THOSE MAGNIFICENT MEN . . .

On the grounds that his battered Curtiss-Robin monoplane, costing £180, was too old, Douglas Corrigan was refused permission by the U.S. authorities to attempt a crossing of the Atlantic in 1937. A year later he took off from New York landing 29½ hours later at Baldonnel Aerodrome near Dublin. His excuse for landing in Ireland instead of California was that his compass was incorrectly set. This picture of "wrong way" Corrigan was taken at Baldonnel.

In the early hours of the morning of April 12, 1928 a Junkers W 33 aircraft, named Bremen, took off from Baldonnel with Col. James C. Fitzmaurice the officer commanding the Irish Army Air Corps at the controls. After what must have seemed a lifetime later, German co-pilot Hermann Koehl guided the machine down onto a snow covered clearing on Greenly Island, Labrador to complete the first East-West crossing of the Atlantic ocean. Fitzmaurice was promoted to the rank of major and given a hero's welcome on his return to Ireland. But

like all the best Irish heroes he was quickly forgotten – until he died in poverty in 1965. Then he was rediscovered briefly while his Tricolour-draped coffin was dispatched to Glasnevin to the accompaniment of the crocodile tears and pious tributes of the assorted dignataries of church and state. ▶

The crew of the Bremen (left to right): Captain Hermann Koehl, Major James C. Fitzmaurice and Gunther Freiherr von Hunefeld.

A brave man was Mr. Selfridge of the famous British store owning family. He pioneered commercial air travel to Ireland. He is seen here saluting the admiring crowds that turned out to greet the first commercial flight – from London to Baldonnel, in June 1919.

Eamonn De Valera had already experienced many testing moments in his extraordinary career, when he first took to the air back in 1936. Fully kitted out for the cold he still looked a trifle wan as he posed for the cameras before takeoff. But he was in safe hands; his pilot was a Colonel Charles Lindbergh, a quite well known and experienced American pilot.

Two advertisements from the early days of Aer Lingus. The sunny way to travel.

This, believe it or not, was the original Aer Lingus terminal at Baldonnel. Passengers could relax in the bars, restaurants or browse in duty free shops while their little DH 84 aeroplane was made ready for the bumpy journey across the Irish Sea.

May 27th 1936 Capt. O.E. Armstrong is happy to be back home after the historic first flight of the Iolar – the entire fleet of Ireland's new national airline, Aer Lingus. The Iolar (Eagle) which carried five passengers was pictured at Baldonnel aerodrome on its return from Bristol. ▶

Honeymooners... at last alone. Well not quite just yet. Back in 1956 eleven newly wed Scottish couples choose Dublin for their first days of married bliss and travelled together on a special Aer Lingus flight from Glasgow. Note the ladies stylish "going away" outfits.

In 1957 debonair Charles Mitchell was a high flying actor who loved to travel on the national airline's popular's Viscount aircraft. He later went on to fame and (we presume) fortune as the chief newsreader on Irish television.

Back in 1946 only the luckiest girls got to fly with Aer Lingus – to such exotic places as Croydon and Bristol. This group of happy hostesses (weren't their little caps cute!) posed on the steps of a reliable old DC 3 – the workhorse of the fleet. ▶

Memories

Sam Stevenson
Architect

*S*tephen's Green is the centre of my Dublin. I have lived and worked in and around it for a good part of my life. It appears to me to be the natural setting for that essential mix of commerce, culture and social intercourse that is the "raison d'etre" of a city. When the Guinness family gave that "Green area of St. Stephen" to the city it was one of many in a long line of benefactions to its citizens that earned the family the affectionate reputation of being very good to the Dubliners. But as Brendan Behan, mindful of his own partiality for the black stuff said in a characteristic piece of Dublin repartee: "So well as they might, for Jasus haven't the Dubliners been very good for the Guinness."

From Leeson Street to Grafton Street and from Baggot Street to Harcourt Street the green forms a stage on which many of Dublin's characters have appeared and performed. I recall seeing Michael MacLiammoir in his latter years walking slowly ahead down Leeson Street. As he approached the corner of the Green he visibly staightened up and, with that ability of a great actor to act with his back, I was aware of the start of another performance, as he launched himself onto the stage of Stephen's Green, and turned towards the Shelbourne for his first scene of the day. Sometimes I would divert from my path to the office and follow him just to hear that magnificent voice, as he greeted his audience of friends by name – Terence! ah! Patrick, or just Darling!

The Shelbourne lounge, a mini theatre of its own, often hosted a cast of performers as varied as Bob Briscoe, Donagh O'Malley, Ted Curtin, Ulick O'Connor, Mary Lavin, Frank O'Connor, Judy Boland, Michael Scott, the Trout Mackey, John Healy, Ben Dunne and many others. These could be seen alone, in pairs or in groups discussing subjects as varied as horses, books, business, art, sex and politics.

Meeting places on the green, where other performances took place, were the D.B.C., the Country Shop and the clubs University, United Services and the Stephen's Green. "Smyths on the Green" for great wine and groceries and the University Church for Byzantine architecture and banal sermons.

The Green has had its bizarre happening – the murder of a young girl above the "Green Tureen" restaurant, and the mutilation and piecemeal disposal of the body in the restaurant refuse. An Indian student, Shan Mohangi – who was convicted of the grizzly crime and subsequently deported – thus earning the Dubliners sobriquet of "No hangi, Mohangi!"

The passing of the Russell Hotel on the south east was a sad loss which has diminished this corner of the green. The dining room, which after the closing of Jammet's Restaurant had the best food and service in Dublin, was decorated by Raymond McGrath in a understated modern style.

In the expansionist decades of the sixties and seventies it was the place to dine and daily it would have its share of performers, artists, actors, businessmen, writers, politicians, bishops, ministers and prime ministers both local and visiting. It had an ambiance which stimulated conversation and on one occasion, when Gore Vidal was one of the lunch guests and himself no mean master of the

"bon mot", he kept repeating "I wish I had said that", in response to remarks made by other guests. This was during, what to me, was an average Irish luncheon conversation.

A story first published in the "New Yorker" recounted a dinner in this restaurant which an Irish politician (Donough O'Malley it turned out to be) had with an elderly blind friend and his guide dog. The friend who had seen better times was unkempt and untidy, but clearly enjoying the good food and wine provided by his host. Towards the end of the meal the waiter brought up the sweet trolley, but O'Malley and friend was in deep conversation, so he did not interrupt and returned to the kitchen. The guide dog who had been ignored up to now, commenced to eat the entire contents of the lower shelf of the dessert trolley, while O'Malley and his guest continued a lively conversation. When O'Malley received his bill, included was a substantial item for the dog's dinner, which he paid after being told what had happened – with the remark "Ah the poor hoor must have been hungry".

A city centre is considered as a series of stages, and its citizens as the performers.

Dublin has had its good share of what are an known as characters. It has been said that the present city lacks such personalities, and I feel it is a common error to assume that the past had a greater store of such individuals. To illustrate this point, I remember my late brother Dan recounting a conversation he overheard in "The Bailey" one late August afternoon between Brendan Behan and Myles Na Gapaleen. Behan who was on the dry, and feeling sorry for himself, was in agreement with Myles about the decline of Dublin life. Myles enquired of Behan what he thought was the problem – "Jaysus! Myles, the trouble with Dublin is that there are no characters left!"

Memories

Brendan Grace
Entertainer

For me there is no place like Dublin. My memories are full and plenty, and above all very happy. I was born and spent my early school days in the Coombe – the heart of the Liberties. We moved from the one-roomed tenement dwelling, when I was nine, to the splendour of far more spacious accommodation on the fourth floor of Echlin Street Buildings, at the heart of Guinness's Brewery. Here was the luxury of two bedrooms, a living room and a scullery; and four floors down, our very own loo!

That was the Dublin I knew. Lots of pals and no shortage of things to do. I was the chief mischief maker in our street. I was a master of crime. We would do the most dreadful things like knocking on people's doors and running like the clappers. Or letting off bangers in the hallways and sometimes even loosening the main fuse in the unlocked fuse boxes on the landings; leaving the poor unfortunate neighbours in the dark. We would then make a few pennies by supplying them with a replacement fuse (which was already there, just loosened) and the day would be saved.

I used to scut on the back of the Guinness horse-and-carts that constantly milled up and down our street with their steel rims hopping off the cobblestones making a deafning racket.

James' Street CBS was literally around the corner from where I lived. So the late Paddy Crosbie's "School around the Corner" had a real significance for me.

I consider myself very fortunate to have had such wonderful parents. We also had the best of neighbours and friends; all of whom I can honestly say made my growing up years special and full of very happy memories.

Like most children then, going to school was anything but pleasant, but I always seemed to fit in enough fun in the classroom to make it acceptable . . . to me and the

pals, that is! Not the teachers!

We had Christian Brothers and a few Masters in James' Street CBS, and they often told my parents that I was a very bright pupil but a mischievious little devil and should concentrate and study more. However, I didn't and subsequently left school at thirteen to work first as a messenger boy and after that . . . everything.

My first job was in the centre of Dublin at two pounds per week, and, wait for it . . . a company bike!! A brand new messenger bike with a big steel carrier in front. Dublin was full of messenger bikes then and we used to race each other down Christchurch hill and do a big skid at the bottom, sometimes shedding the load of parcels being carried in the front and earning a good telling off by the poor unfortunate customer whose delivery was wrecked.

Dublin had its great characters like Bang Bang who chased after buses and stood on the bus platform with a big key pointing at us and shouting BANG! Very harmless and very entertaining and most of all, respected by the youth of the day.

There was Razor Blade, a small hunchbacked man with a patch over one eye and always unshaven. ("Today it's called 'designer stubble'). He always stood at the corner of Christchurch and Nicholas Street and again was quite harmless.

I remember another man called "The Count". He was a real gentleman tramp. Now I use the word 'tramp' with the utmost respect. He would walk along the Clanbrassil Street area with a top hat, a cane and always a fresh

flower in his lapel. He looked most distinguished.

I was up Nelson's Pillar (don't correct me please and say it was Nelson Pillar with no 's'). We all called it Nelson's. Going up was okay, but coming down was a nightmare, especially if you met someone coming up. I remember one day meeting a big fat woman half way, she was coming down . . . backwards. She had run out of puff and couldn't turn around, so we all had to back her down and she was screaming like a divil.

When Dublin lost its traffic cops it was a tragedy. The men in blue along the River Liffey at O'Connell Bridge were great characters. I got to know them quite well on my rounds as a delivery boy. Besides, my Da used to serve them with soup and creamy pints as a barman in Phil O'Reilly's in Hawkins Street – just opposite the old Theatre Royal. He was Seamus Grace, the most popular and best loved pint puller in Dublin.

Phil O'Reillys' was a hive of activity and had a super atmosphere. It had a saloon bar for men and a cocktail lounge for men and women. My Dad used to get "briefs" for the Regal and the Royal. I saw my first ever movie in the Regal Rooms and my first ever stage show in the Royal. My Mammy used bring me into town on the number twenty one bus. We'd meet Dad after his half day and into the Royal. All the ushers knew my Dad, and I would always be sure of sweets and chocolate as we went in. My sister Maria missed all this, she was only a baby.

The times change alright and dear old Dublin has changed alright, almost, at times, beyond recognition. But for me memories linger. I'm sorry for my own children, who never met Bang Bang, never saw the Pillar or the Royal, or even a real messenger boy's bike; or a fire brigade with a bell ringing instead of a siren.

Ah yes, Pete St. John said it for us all: "I'll remember Dublin City in the rare auld times".

"Do you remember? Will I ever forget." Two Dublin Ladies in 1952-53.

Tinkers, happily encamped in a traditional caravan at Del Monte Place, off Gardiner Street in 1952-53.

The flapping clothes are guaranteed to slow the traffic down as it passes through Masterson's Lane. ▶

An extensive range of junk for sale at the romantically named Engine Alley.

"It's a two-pocket apron for some fishy profits" Moore Street in the 1950's.

"But would they be good for dancing?". Shoes galore at Anglesea Market. ▶

"Get the last of the ripe bananas."

"A right bunch of tulips." Moore Street, in the heart of Dublin is famous for it's outdoor stalls selling fruit and vegetables and fish. The street traders are renowned for the wit and humour and the cheerful banter of commerce is one of the great attractions of this bustling street.

"How many will I get love?" ▶

The Guinness Brewery was started by Arthur Guinness in 1759 at St. James Gate. For over two hundred years, the business has remained in the Guinness family and the fame of Guinness stout is worldwide. The company has always been regarded as a generous employer and generations of families worked inside the walls of the great brewery, during its long history.

Coopers pause at their work for this picture, which was taken in Bow Lane, Dublin in 1918.

This ornate transport vehicle, which dates from 1895, was known as a pair-horse wagon.

Endless barrels of porter. A Dublin man's dream, photographed in 1925. ▶

UNCLE ARTHUR'S BREW

This handsome Guinness float was entered in the Dublin St. Patrick's Day Parade of 1938.

Throughout its history, Guinness have always encouraged visitors to the brewery. This visitors train was introduced in 1875. Here a group of visitors enjoy the ride in 1886.

A steaming barge carries hogshead of export Guinness down the Liffey to Dublin Port. The barges were often subjected to Dublin wits crying "bring us back a parrot." ▶

The original Abbey Theatre, which also housed the Peacock Theatre. It was destroyed by fire on July 18, 1951 and the company moved to the Queens Theatre, a famous variety theatre in Pearse Street. The Queens remained the home of the Abbey until July 9, 1961, when the new Abbey was reopened on the original site in Abbey Street.

The Capitol Cinema in Princess Street, had a variety show coupled with a movie as its entertainment. A spectacular organ which rose from the pit, was one of the main attractions. The BHS Store now occupies the site.

The Metropole Ballroom in Dublin was a famous dance venue. The building, which occupied the site of the British Home Stores in O'Connell Street, also housed a cinema and many romances had their beginnings inside and outside "the Met." ▶

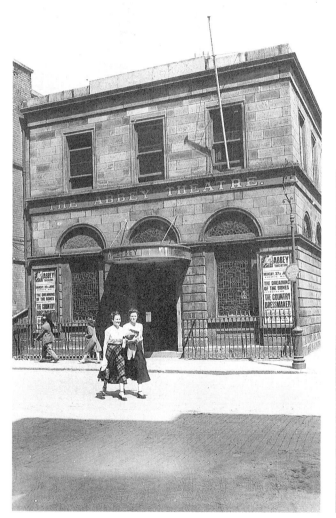

Every onion in this shop in Summerhill has had a medical check-up.

Mining for literary gems at the O'Connell Bridge Bookstall.

A lot of statues to move. The Zenith Statue company's workshop at St. Kevin's cottages. ▶

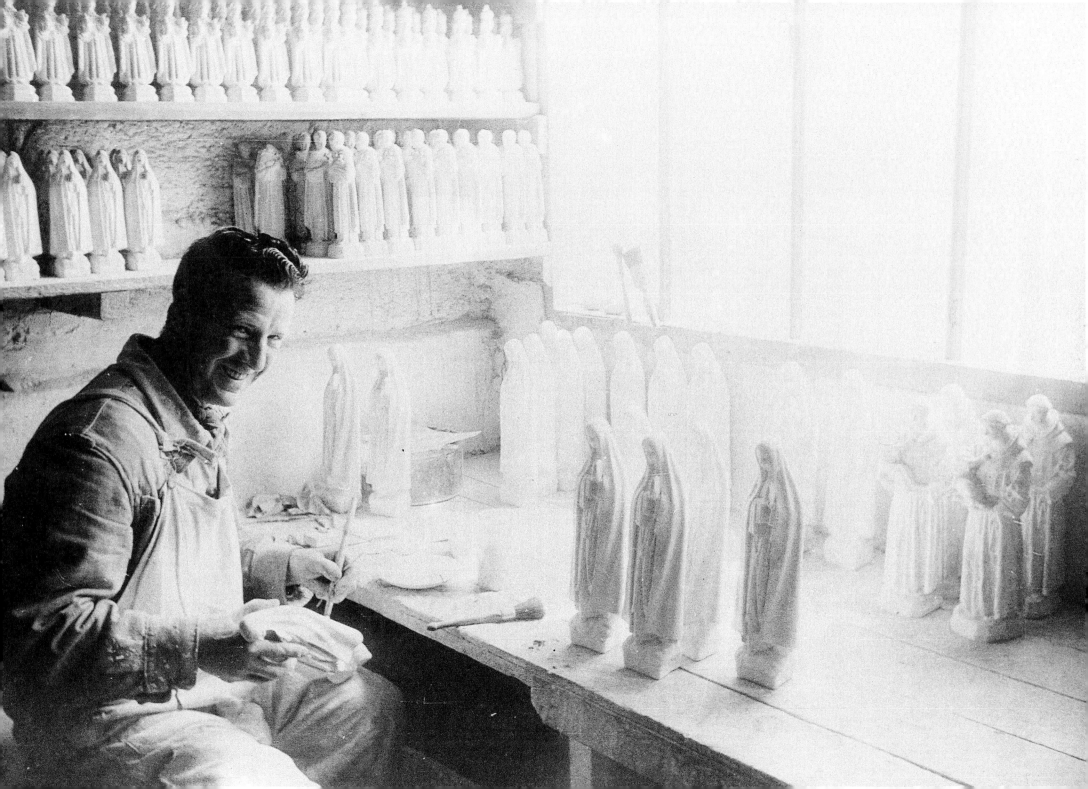

"Good morning Sister." Dominick Street in 1952.

"Two plain, one purl." Outdoor knitting on the steps of a tenement in Gardiner Street.

The Ha'penny Bridge spanning the Liffey just south of O'Connell Bridge, was once a toll-bridge for pedestrians. It is still a vital link between the North and the South city. ▶

"Give us a push Mister." A Dublin city children's playground in the 1950's.

"There's a big one." St. Stephen's Green. Children play in the heart of the city in the 1950's.

"Did ja never see a horse before?" Patrick Street in the 50's. ▶

A glass of porter and a witty exchange. A nostalgic reminder of a Dublin pub in the 1950's.

The horse-drawn delivery van was still an everyday sight on the streets of Dublin in the 1950's.

"I've got a bird here going cheep." Dublin Bird Market in the 1950's. ▶

Christmas 1953. The Royal Hibernian Hotel in Dawson Street stands resplendant. It was since been demolished and replaced by the new Royal Hibernian Way shopping mall.

The Long Hall Bar in South Great George's Street wears it's decorations proudly. Long Hall is still one of Dublins most individual bars.

"Sing out, you're being watched." Carol singing in 1953. ▶

VINCENT
DE PAUL,
"LITTLE FLOWER"
CONFERENCE,
DONORE AVENUE.
COLLECTION
SOCIETY OF ST. VINCENT DE PAUL
CAROL SINGERS COLLECTION
SOCIETY OF ST. VINCENT DE PAUL

The frozen pond at Dublin Zoo proves irresistible for skaters on March 1st 1947.

The official opening of the Lion House (Roberts House) in 1902. Field Marshall Earl Roberts was President of the Society 1898–1902.

The Dublin Zoological Gardens in the Phoenix Park were opened to the public in September 1831. The front gate lodge was erected shortly after, in 1832. ▶

THE ZOO-O-LOGICAL GARDENS

The camel house and enclosure in 1917.

Sara the Elephant, who lived from 1932-1962, was the last elephant to give daily rides on the main walk at Dublin Zoo. With her is Ceylonese elephant Komali.

The house in the background was built to accommodate a giraffe in 1845. When the giraffe died the elephants moved into the house, until it was replaced by the present house, which was built in 1956.

Male elephant Rama, with his Keeper McNally and trainer Capt. Harrington. The Keeper, McNally, was killed by an elephant in 1903. ▶

Dr. Terry Murphy, who joined the Zoo in 1948 as an Assistant Superintendent and went on to become the much loved public face of the Zoo until his retirement in 1984.

President Erskine Childers and his wife make the acquaintance of a new puma cub during an official presidential visit to the Zoo.

In 1976, Hilda the hippotamus proved more than a match for the crate that was being used to transport her to Longleat Safari Park in England. Hilda, who weighed more than two tons, bent the $2\frac{1}{2}''$ thick bars on the front of the crate and made a daring dash back into the pond in her enclosure. ▶

Memories

David Norris
Academic

Dublin, although not strictly the City of my birth, is the source of my earliest conscious memories. When I open the Pandora's Box of recollection, out streams an insistent flock of images stretching back to infant recollections of the late 40's.

Trams (open topped in summer on the Dalkey route) sailing majestically into town along tree lined Northumberland Road – but how treacherous were those self same tracks for unwary cyclists, trying desperately to keep wobbling machines upright and out of their imprisoning grooves, as we pedalled up to Herbert Park with jam-jars and pinkeen nets over the handlebars.

For these expeditions we could buy bamboo rods, with small hooped nets at one end, in Herbert House in Ballsbridge from which also the Irish Times was delivered – (four old pence an issue!) by a nervous fleet footed adolescent. Those were the days when things were delivered, and before the advent of the supermarkets, two great grocery stores, Findlaters and Leverett & Fryes had branches in all the suburbs of Dublin.

In our village of Sandymount both had floors strewn with sawdust, and a particular grocery smell compounded from the odours of individual counters which sold cheese, spices, biscuits (including the now vanished broken biscuits and café noir) in batteries of glass lidded metal boxes, fruit, dish, meat and vegetables.

Cash purchasers had the pleasure of watching their change skating along the ceiling on a network of wires in little hollow containers, but everyday those shops also telephoned our mothers respectfully to take the day's order for delivery. At Christmas time the larger Dublin shops sent magical illustrated catalogues of food, toys and luxury goods and in Pims of George's Street, now vanished, there was the most wonderful Santa Claus on earth.

The war was a recent memory and most suburban back gardens had – although Ireland was neutral – air raid shelters, which became the focus for forbidden domestic adventure. In our cul' de' sac in Ballsbridge we could pelt – in relative safety – down the road on skates whose steel wheels struck sparks from the concrete; hopping onto the pavement to avoid Johnson Mooney's bread van and stopping ourselves by reaching out and swinging around one of those graceful swan-necked street lamps, a few of which still survive.

How simple our childhood pleasures seem now! What excitement it was when one of our friends' parents drove us into the Dublin Docks to watch the B&I Boat set out each evening for Liverpool, or even more daring if we walked in through Ringsend and took the ferry across the Liffey walking out along the south wall, past the Pigeon House to our destination of the Poolbeg Lighthouse. And then there was the Spring Show at the R.D.S., where it seemed as if every child in Ireland had flooded into the

Exhibition Halls to collect souvenirs and a mass of incomprehensible leaflets on tractors and milking machines and badges advertising everything from the latest radio set to the national transport network.

During term time Dublin was full of school children; many schools still being located at that time in the city centre. I was a boarder at St. Andrew's College in Clyde Road and later a day boy at the High School in gently curving Georgian Harcourt Street, both now banished to the area beyond Dublin's two encircling canals.

On Saturday afternoons we went to the cinema – cowboy and gangster films at the Carlton in O'Connell Street; meeting up at Nelson's Pillar (am I the only Dubliner ever to have climbed it and seen the city's roofscape from its top?) or, if an older sister or brother took us, to the Theatre Royal where Tommy Dando and his wurlitzer rose from the floor with electronic ease to accompany our massed voices, while a little white dot bounced over the words of familiar songs on the screen.

There was something distinctive about Dublin in those days which I hope and believe has not been entirely lost. Guinness Boats on the Liffey and the distinctive malty scent of the brewery on the air, cobblestones and canal barges, handsom cabs and kids playing hopscotch and our own larger-than-life characters, Jimmy O'Dea and Maureen Potter in pantomine and Brendan Behan acting out the tragic pantomine of his own life, interrupting his own plays at the Queens Theatre with his inimitable singing of The Old Triangle.

Dublin had character and characters then, I am a middle aged optimist and I believe it still has both in a greater degree than any other capital but then I am biased. If J.F.K. could say to applause "Ich bin ein Berliner" – then I say with equal pride – Ich bin ein Dubliner.

Memories

Garret FitzGerald
Former Taoiseach

*A*s the great-grandson of a Dubliner, who was educated at the Model School in the early years of the last century, albeit one who migrated back to his family's native Kerry later in life, I suppose I have one slightly deeper root in Dublin than many other citizens of this city. Over a century after that great-grandfather's birth, my parents came – from Kerry – to live near, and then in, Dublin. For myself, I was born here, have lived here, will remain here, will die here, if I can manage it, and will be buried here. I couldn't visualise ever living anywhere else.

I suppose that one's attachment to one's native city is a function both of one's lifetime memories of it, and of the people one has known there over the years. The past and the people. Is it perhaps the case that the more a city changes, the more one's memories of it are nostalgic, and therefore powerful?

If so, Dublin has done a lot to make it citizens attached to it – for few cities which escaped wartime destruction have lost so much of their past through neglect, through vandalism, through bad management, inadequate planning and sheer greed. Those of us who are native Dubliners are inclined to blame blow-ins for what we have lost, but I suppose we have to admit that it wasn't all culchies that did the harm. Dubliners themselves have neglected their city. Sometimes I dream of an immense oil bonanza that would not alone solve our economic and social problems but would also enable us to knock down excrescences like the ESB building in Fitzwilliam Street and livingly re-build, as skilfully and beautifully as our ancestors first built the Georgian dwellings that were destroyed to make way for these shoddy modern blocks.

Sometimes, more modestly I dream of architects being given the opportunity to design some fine buildings for our city in the future; too often they have been given such a financially restrictive brief that they have not been able to exercise their talents to create worthwhile structures – which some, at least, of them have the capacity to do.

A millennium celebration won't give us the chance to do much along these lines. What it could, and should do, is provide the incentive to clean up our city, and to keep it clean thereafter. A tidy second thousand years? Perhaps. Perhaps not. And could the financially hard-pressed Corporation find the means of doing, in the Millennial Year, what the rapidly-abolished Streets Commission was planning to do with our centre city – to restore what is left of the city's core to a reasonable condition in terms of signs and street furniture, traffic control and pedestrian freedom? Perhaps. Perhaps not.

I think that in any event it's a year during which we are entitled to give our nostalgia free rein: to remember the tall swaying trams stopping to set down and pick up passengers on O'Connell Bridge, as the smoke from the Guinness barges, their funnels lowered as they passed under the bridge at high tide, puffed up through the gratings in the traffic islands. To remember the bright colours of the very miscellaneous vehicles operated by the many bus companies before these concerns – with the

single exception of the St. Kevins Bus to Glendalough – were extinguished by the railway company and DUTC monopolies. To remember also the frilly-capped waitresses in Grafton Street's Mitchells, serving the flat round sandwich cakes, the silver-iced cherry-topped German biscuits and the sponge cakes whose distinctive flavour could be enhanced, when no one was looking, by buttering them.

To remember also the wooden blocks that paved Grafton Street, the Georgian elegance of the eastern and southern sides of St. Stephen's Green; to remember the Drumm battery train and the high-funnelled steam engines of the 1880's that plied in competition with it on the two lines to Bray; to remember Switzer's lending library; the river full of shipping up to the Custom House – including the schooner with its tall mast that plied from Bristol to Butt Bridge until the 1950's; the rough grass of the meadow in Parnell Square – the Memorial Garden is there now – where during the War, as members of the LDG, we crawled on our stomachs to see how near we could get to the 'enemy' without being observed.

Memories of places, memories of family friends, people like Sarah Purser, born in the first half of the last century, to whose monthly salon in Mespil House, long since destroyed, I was just too young to be invited before she died. And Edward and Christine Longford in the Gate; Ernest Blythe in the Abbey.

But then, all this represented only the last few decades of a thousand years – give or take a few. We're only the last of many generations to bemoan what's gone. Our children will have different memories; I hope their quite different memories will tie them as tightly to their native city as we have been tied by ours. And so on, for the next millennium.

President Kennedy makes his historic address to the Irish parliament in Leinster House. The Taoiseach of that time, Sean Lemass, sits with his hands clasped (bottom right).

A hero's welcome awaited President John F. Kennedy when he paid a visit to the land of his ancestors in June 1963.

Flanked by police and military, President Kennedy takes the accolades of Dublin's citizens as he drives down O'Connell Street with President Eamonn De Valera.▶

The President of Ireland, Sean T. O'Ceallaigh, greets
Cardinal Cushing of New York, when he paid a visit in
1965, a year before the death of the president.

Prince Albert and Princess Caroline of Monaco are
instantly recognisable, as children in this charming
photograph taken with Sile Bean De Valera during a
visit to Ireland by Princess Grace in June 1961.

A radiant Princess Grace with Bean de Valera during her
1961 visit to Ireland. ▶

On March 8, 1966 (the 50th anniversary year of the
Easter Rising) Dublin said goodbye to The Pillar,
suddenly. Those responsible for blowing it up were never
apprehended. The army demolished what was left in a
controlled explosion.

When Gladstone lost the British elections of 1886 on the issue of the Home Rule Bill for Ireland, it was a defeat that spelt victory for Charles Stuart Parnell, the Irish statesman, whose statue stands proudly at the top of O'Connell Street. Parnell was the first Irishman to win acknowledgement of the possibility of Home Rule. His final years as a public figure were marred by scandal of an extramarital relationship with Kitty O'Shea, wife of a former colleague of Parnell's. The ten year affair ended in marriage when Kitty O'Shea was finally divorced in 1891; but five months later on October 6th, 1891 Parnell died.

President Eamon De Valera gives the graveside oration at the re-interrment of Sir Roger Casement at Glasnevin Cemetry on March 1st, 1965. Casement had been convicted of treason and hanged at Pentonville prison on August 3rd, 1916 and after years of negotiation the Irish patriots remains were repatriated to Ireland, where he was accorded a full State funeral.

Last honours for Eamon De Valera, regarded as the finest Statesman in Modern Irish history. He fought in the 1916 Rising and having opposed the Treaty, he went on to form the Fianna Fail party in 1926. He served in public office for sixty-three years, eventually becoming President of Ireland. He died, August 29th, 1975. ▶

The confident smile was there from the beginning. Gay Byrne, our most famous media personality in his early days as a radio broadcaster.

This joker grew to love the microphone. And the cameras. Terry Wogan hams it up as a young radio broadcaster in Radio Eireann.

The cream of comedy. Jimmy O'Dea (left) is still remembered for his roguish humour, especially his great creation, Biddy Mulligan the Pride of the Coombe. Next to him is Maureen Potter, who assumed Jimmy's mantle, to become Ireland's premier comedienne. Harry O'Donovan (behind) wrote most of Jimmy O'Dea's famous sketches. Danny Cummins (right) was a perfect foil for O'Dea, as well as being a fine comedian in his own right. ▶

RADIO DAYS

Mairead Ní Ghrada, was the first female announcer on Radio Éireann. Joe Linnane (right) went on to fame as an Abbey actor and radio personality.

"Din Joe", in real life Denis Fitzgibbon, was part of the golden era of radio, with his programme "Take The Floor." Here he shares a gag with fellow commedians Al Thomas (centre) and Jack Cruise (right).

That was a bit discordant lads! A pep talk for Paul Russell and the Viscounts from Radio Eireann's Kevin Roche (for many years head of light entertainement) while a younger Gaybo listens attentively. Paul Russell later became the first presenter of "The Showband Show" on Irish television. In the 1960's Showbands were to Ireland what the Beatles were to the rest of the world. ▶

President Eamonn De Valera addresses the Irish nation on the commencement of the national television service Radio Telefis Eireann on December 31st, 1961.

It was someone elses life the night RTE television began, but Eamonn Andrews host to "This Is Your Life," had the surprised look of a man who had just caught sight of the famous red book.

Outside the Gresham Hotel in O'Connell Street, Patrick O'Hagan, father of Irish Eurovision winner Johnny Logan, entertains the throng who have gathered to celebrate the opening night of RTE. Note the solitary television for the crowd. ▶

When Bob Geldof and the Boomtown Rats played their last gig at Moran's Hotel in Talbot Street Dublin and set off to find fame and fortune in England, few could have envisaged just how famous Geldof would become as a rockstar, as a humanitarian and as a world celebrity.

For the past twenty-five years, the name of The Dubliners has spread around the music world, as the famous bearded folk group carried Irish music and song to foreign audiences, filling the joint role of musicians and ambassadors for Dublin. Included in the photograph is the late Luke Kelly, for many years one of the most famous and talented members of the group.

Dickie Rock was Dublin's most successful showband star. Back in the 1960's, the versatile showbands attracted huge crowds to the dance halls which mushroomed all over Ireland to accommodate their fans. Dickie, who sang with the Miami Showband, is now a successful cabaret artist.

Croke Park Stadium, headquarters of the Gaelic Athletic Association proved the perfect venue for the triumphant homecoming concerts by Dublin's most famous rock band, U2 in 1987. The warmth of the crowd's welcome and the response of the band members, Bono, The Edge, Larry Mullins and Adam Clayton turned the event into a joyous celebration of the capital city. ▶

The visit by Pope John Paul II to Ireland in September 1979, was an historic moment for Irish Catholics. In an astonishing display of warmth and fervour over one million people, almost one third of the population, attended the Papal Mass at the Phoenix Park in Dublin.

The big moment. Pope John Paul II sets foot (almost) on Irish soil.

A farewell wave from his Holiness. Cardinal Tomas O Fiach is his fellow-passenger. ▶

President Richard Milhouse Nixon and his wife Pat, arrive on Air Force One for an official visit to Ireland on October 3rd, 1970.

Jack Swiggert, Fred Haise and James Lovell, the three astronauts from Apollo XIII, paraded through the streets of Dublin as part of President Richard Nixon's entourage.

President Ronald Reagan and his wife Nancy, with President Patrick Hillery and his wife Maeve, during Reagan's visit to Ireland in 1984, when he addressed both houses of the Oireachtas. ▶

Dr. A.J.F. "Tony" O'Reilly, in flying style, on the wing for the Irish rugby union team in 1956. Now the Chief Executive of the giant Heinz Corporation, and chairman of Independent Newspapers in Ireland. O'Reilly won 29 caps for Ireland between 1955-1970.

Harry "The Brad" Bradshaw is the famous professional at Portmarnock Golf Club, on Dublin's northside. Along with Christy O'Connor, Bradshaw won the Canada Cup (now known as the World Cup), in Mexico in 1958. Bradshaw was famous for his no nonsense style of "knock-em-in" putting.

Dublin's second great football team became known as Heffo's Army in the first half of the 1970's. Massive crowds of Dubliners flocked to the famous Hill 16 at Croke Park, to cheer on the Dublin team and the tremendous vocal support from the supporters was a much feared weapon in the Dublin armoury. Urging on the crowd is the portly Dublin full forward Jimmy Keavney, who was Dublin's most feared marksman. ▶

The Irish Rugby Union Team, led by Ciarain Fitzgerald 1985, won the Triple Crown, beating England, Scotland, and Wales. On the left in this picture is Fergus Slattery, Ireland's wing forward who played for Ireland sixty one times, as well as winning honours with the British and Irish Lions.

Famous Irish athlete Eamon Coghlan, returns in triumph to Dublin Airport, having won the 5000M at the inaugural World Championships at Helsinki in 1983.

Stephen Roche from Dundrum electrified the whole world with his cycling exploits in 1987 when he won the Tour of Italy, the Tour De France and the World Cycling Championship. He was made a Freeman of Dublin and on his triumphant return from his famous Tour De France victory he was given a victory parade through the city in an open-topped bus. ▶

DUBLIN BUS
BRINGS STEPHEN
HOME

Liam Brady made his mark in British football with London club, Arsenal. He moved to Italy for a spell before returning to play with West Ham in the English League. He is currently a member of the Irish soccer team.

All-Ireland Football Final 1963. Dublin v Galway. Action near the Galway goal in the 1963 All-Ireland Football Final, during the first great era of Dublin football. Players from left are, Sean Meade (G), Simon Behan (D), John Donnellan (G), Noel Tierney (G), Des (Snitchy) Ferguson (D), Enda Colleran (G), Mickey Whelan (D) and Noel Fox (D).

Red deer gaze calmly at onlookers in the snowy tranquility of the Phoenix Park. The herd of deer roams freely through the park, mostly in the areas close to the Chapelizod and Islandbridge gates, on the western side. ▶

On St. Valentine's Day, 1981, a disastrous fire at the Stardust Disco in Artane, took the lives of 45 young people. Two more died later. The grief was felt nationwide as the true horror of the decimation of families unfolded. The Stardust Disaster was the single biggest accidental loss of life in Dublin this century.

The still, broad majesty of O'Connell Street can be seen in this shot taken from the corner of Westmoreland Street in 1986. ▶

A stretch of Liffey skyline dominated by contrasting architectural styles. The controversial Dublin Civic Offices stand in front of Christchurch Cathedral. There was a church on this site in 1038; building started on the present structure in 1172.

Time is frozen in this 1987 snowscape in the grounds of Trinity College. ▶

Tailors Hall in Back Lane, was originally a row of houses. It was purchased by the merchant tailors of Dublin at the end of the seventeenth century and converted to a guild hall.

The arch was built in 1714. The hall was saved from demolition in the 1970's and restored. In 1984 it became the headquarters of An Taisce, the Irish National Trust and it is also currently in use as a venue for conferences and entertainments.

The timeless nature of this candid portrait belies its modern vintage. The photograph was taken in 1982.

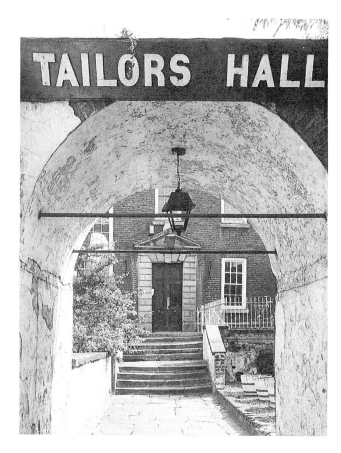